FIND OUT BY TOUCHING

FIND OUT

BY TOUCHING

by **PAUL SHOWERS**
illustrated by **ROBERT GALSTER**

REC ® LIBRARY EDITION

THOMAS Y. CROWELL COMPANY · NEW YORK

LET'S-READ-AND-FIND-OUT SCIENCE BOOKS

Editors: *DR. ROMA GANS*, Professor Emeritus of Childhood Education, Teachers College, Columbia University

DR. FRANKLYN M. BRANLEY, Chairman and Astronomer of The American Museum–Hayden Planetarium

*AVAILABLE IN SPANISH

L.C. Card No. 60-13242

ISBN 0-690-29781-5
0-690-29782-3 (LB)

REC Library Edition reprinted with the permission of Thomas Y. Crowell Company

Responsive Environments Corp., Englewood Cliffs, N. J. 07632

U.S. 1801965

FIND OUT BY TOUCHING

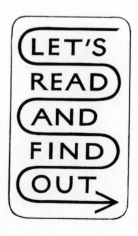

Touch the carpet. How does it feel?

Touch this page. How does it feel?
Touch the window. How does it feel?

5

Touch your face. How does it feel?

The carpet is rough.

The page is smooth.

The window is cold.

Your face is warm.
Each feels different.

You know that they are different because you touched
 them.
You discover many things by touching.
You do not always have to see things to know what
 they are.

Let's play a game.
The game will show what you can discover by
 touching.

It takes two people to play this game.
Play the game with your friend.
You and your friend take turns.
You will need a big box to play this game.
Put different things in the box.

11

Put in some things made of wood.

Have you a pencil? Put in the pencil.

Have you a wooden top? Put in the top.

Have you a stick? Put in the stick.

If you have no pencil or top or stick, put in other things made of wood.

Now put in some things made of metal.

Have you a key? Put in the key.

Have you a nail? Put in the nail.

Have you a spoon? Put in the spoon.

If you have no key or nail or spoon, put in other things made of metal.

15

Put in some things made of cloth.

Can you get a washcloth?

Do you have a scarf?

Put them into the box.

Ask your mother for a piece of cloth. An old stocking
will do.

Put that into the box, too.

Next put in some different kinds of things:

    a plastic dish and a plastic toy,

    a stone, a piece of chalk, a leaf,

    an eraser, a nut, a brush, a balloon.

If you have none of these things, use other things in

    their place:

    a sponge, or a comb, or a piece of cotton.

Put in all sorts of things: string, or marbles, even a

    potato.

Now you have a box full of many different things.

Mix them up.

Now you are ready to play your game. If your turn comes first, shut your eyes. Reach into the box and pick out something.

Feel it.
What is it? Can you tell?
No peeking.

What is it made of?

    Is it wood?

    Is it cloth?

    Is it metal?

How does it feel?

    Is it smooth?

    Is it rough?

    Is it cold?

    Is it warm?

What is it?

Maybe you can tell by the way it feels.

Tell your friend what you think it is.

Do not peek. Your friend will tell you if you are right.

Now it is your friend's turn.

He keeps his eyes shut. He reaches into the box.
He picks out something.

What do his fingers tell him?

Is it a stone?

Is it a brush?

Is it a potato?

What is it? How does it feel?

What does your friend think it is?

You tell him if he is right or wrong.

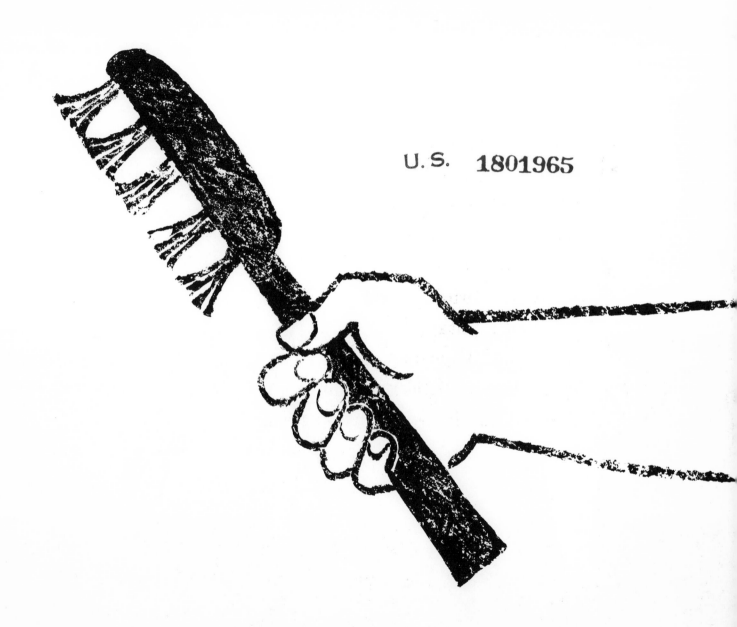

U.S. 1801965

25

Take turns playing this game.
How many times are you right?
How many times is he right?
How many times are you wrong?
How many times is he wrong?

You and your friend will be right most of the time.

Your fingers tell you the right answer.

Your fingers tell you if things are hard or soft.

Your fingers tell you if things are cold or warm, rough or smooth.

Your fingers tell you many things.
A plastic dish is smooth, hard, and cold.
Your fingers tell you so.
A kitten is soft, and warm, and furry.
Your fingers tell you so.

You do not always have to see a thing to know what
   it is.
You can feel what it is with your fingers.
You learn about things by touching them.

33

33

Today your fingers will touch many things.
What will your fingers tell you?

ABOUT THE AUTHOR

PAUL SHOWERS is a New York newspaperman and writer of more than a dozen books for children. He first became interested in making books for young readers after watching his own children struggle with the "See, Sally, see" books of the 1950's ("television's greatest boon," he calls them). His own books, most of them in the Let's-Read-and-Find-Out series, have thoroughly proved that children's books can be both lively and worth while.

Mr. Showers began newspaper work on the Detroit *Free Press*. Then came the New York *Herald Tribune*, a brief stint on the New York *Sunday Mirror* and, for the past twenty-five years, the Sunday *New York Times*. Mr. Showers was born in Sunnyside, Washington, and has an A.B. degree from the University of Michigan.

ABOUT THE ARTIST

ROBERT GALSTER has illustrated books for children as well as an adult novel. He has designed book jackets and record album covers and has painted murals for hotels in New York, Boston, and Florida. Mr. Galster is perhaps best known for his poster designs for the Broadway theater. He first became interested in poster design while he served with the Army Engineers in Europe. Mr. Galster is a native of the Illinois farm belt and grew up in Mansfield, Ohio. He now lives in New York City, where he formerly attended the Parsons School of Design.